THE BEST OF BEARDSLEY

AUBREY   BEARDSLEY

THE BEST

OF

BEARDSLEY

collected and edited by

R. A. WALKER

EXCALIBUR BOOKS

Contents

Foreword

THE selection of the drawings as being the best work of the artist is the personal one of the Editor. It is in fact an anthology of drawings, but like all anthologies, whether of flowers, poems or pictures, it has the merit of its defects. It might have included many more, for one reason or another, and it might have omitted many others. But a choice is a decision which will inevitably leave some to mourn the omission of a drawing, whilst it is hoped others will welcome a design they have not lately seen.

A number of cover designs has been included as Beardsley was probably, with Charles Ricketts, the best designer of these in the period when he worked. The Editor subscribes to the fashionable slogan of "fitness for purpose", as eagerly as the hypochondriac takes the latest drug—while it cures.

The omission of Morte Darthur drawings is because these were the work of his 'prentice hands, and the present volume is not intended to demonstrate the rapid development of his genius. *Quod erat inveniendum.*

R.A.W.

The Art of Aubrey Beardsley

THE art of Aubrey Beardsley is *hors concours*. It belongs to no school nor tradition, to no age nor period. Indeed, has not Max Beerbohm, born the same month and year, said he belongs to "The Beardsley period"? And the Airy Max is still with us, pale possibly, but always gaily loitering. Yet Beardsley has been dead for half a century!

It is this paradox that makes it hard to classify Beardsley. He is a modern, yet he was dead before Walter Sickert or Augustus John had been heard of by the general public.

His work belongs, perhaps, to that rare kind of limbo of the aesthetic stratosphere to which might be assigned the Preludes to Wagner's Operas, the pencil heads of John, the paintings of William Maris or of Leonardo, some of the piano music of Chopin, the poetry of Keats and the Fêtes Champêtres of Watteau. The cold purity of their perfection seems to ban the emotion they arouse.

Like Aeschylus and Mr. Williams he has indeed "created the taste by which he is to be enjoyed". His art was new at the time of its making, it is still new to-day, though more familiar to us : he has now created that taste. His followers, or rather his imitators, have never really grasped his essential quality, the cold, clear, biting line, the perfection of balance in his design, his amazing economy of beautiful detail, his daring use of black and white mass and his unerring instinct for correct values.

That such rare and important qualities should be found all together in one draftsman is most unusual. But that they should be allied to great intelligence, a ready wit, a sardonic humour and an erotic temperament is probably unique.

It is this alliance of craftsmanship and character that makes Beardsley at once so easy and so difficult to criticize. Every drawing of his maturity gives evidence of his individual way of looking at a subject, whether it be a Victorian interior, a Greek play, an eighteenth-century poem, a woman looking at some books, an early seventeenth-century satire, or an airy nothing—an amour being interred in a powder box by a pierrot and a satyr.

Beside his extreme youth and maturity, another paradox is noticeable. He was most sensitive to the zeitgeist of the later Victorians. Not a foible, fashion or custom was missed by that acute mind : the Burne-Jones craze, the yellow-backed French novel, the Japanese print, the Whistler nocturne and the Whistler peacock room. He saw the uproarious posters of Chéret, the poster-like lithographs of Toulouse-Lautrec, the woodcuts of Charles Ricketts, the garish gaslit London streets. He heard the mot of Oscar and the gibe of Jimmy at the critics.

All these, and a dozen other tricks and fancies, he observed and transmuted into his own design and made something as distinctive as a Chinese bronze of the Warring States, or a modern ballet by Massine.

To realize the complete originality of his technique, one must turn to the popular black and white artists of his day, such as Railton or Pennell. These and many other artists before and after them have used their pens as if they were writing. They do not draw, they write their pictures. Their work is a mass of wiry, nervous, scribbling, sometimes effective, more often not. For instance the many architectural drawings of Railton seem to have no masonry in them. A famous Gothic church tower arises, delicate and slightly vague from a mass of irrelevant detail—to make an ineffective vignette or chapter-heading. The whole thing is fussy and overwrought. Compare them to any architectural detail or background in Beardsley's work, and it will be seen how sharp and clear and planned his work is.

It is the difference rather between engraving and etching. Our artist would have made a natural engraver. All lines are clear cut or graved and do not depend on cross hatching or shading for effect. The amazing strength of outline, balanced with solid black, must and does tell the whole story.

If there was any contemporary artist from whom he learnt any of his technique it was Phil May, who has not hitherto been mentioned by other critics; Phil May certainly had the same facility, with a single line, of expressing dramatic gesture or emotion, be it only a gentleman pub-crawler or a slightly inebriated charwoman.

Throughout his life, Beardsley was more influenced by literary, than human, contacts, and it may safely be said that one book taught him more than all his contemporaries. That book was the Morte Darthur. Early in 1893 he entered into the contract with Mr. J. M. Dent, then a young and pushing publisher, under which he supplied over 350 separate designs, and he was under 21 when he made the contract! The payments he received set him free from the uncongenial task of an insurance clerk and he set to with a will.

The earliest drawings, both full-page and border designs, are exceedingly elaborate and complex, not to say confused. But at this rate he would never have fulfilled his contract, as there was a time element, the book being issued in parts. So with time against him (as it was throughout his disease-troubled life) and a quick and instinctive appreciation of his medium he made his drawings broader, and simpler, using great cunning in black and white space to save himself time and trouble. In this connection it is of interest to know that his paternal grandfather has been described in official documents as manufacturing goldsmith, jeweller, or working goldsmith. So an instinct for the right use of his medium was probably inherited. Even so, the contract for so young and intelligent a man was a gruelling one and therefore one of two things was bound to happen. Either he would become a mere hack, turning out ingenious, but ever-feebler grotesques, ornaments and border designs, or there would be a violent reaction against all mediaevalism, Morte Darthur god-wottery and Wardour Street Morris. This reaction took place. And so it is that in April 1893, in the first number of The Studio appeared such a drawing as J'ai baisé ta bouche Iokanaan, the first version of The Climax, and made before he started the Salome contract for John Lane.

For a time he led a Jekyll and Hyde existence, turning out vignettes for the interminable Morte Darthur in the fake wood-cut style and at the same time indulging his fancy and imagination in drawings which show more of a Japanese than a mediaeval influence.

Actually the Morte Darthur contract was a blessing in disguise, as most blessings are. Without it he might have become diffuse and dilatory. He would certainly have tried other mediums, and indeed his sole essay in oils is in the Tate Gallery. But from constant practice with india ink, he became more proficient than any living artist. Its difficulties and delicacies were clear to him, and his reaction saved us from witnessing a steady downward trend in an illustrated Faery Queen, Aucassin or Mabinogion.

He had served his apprenticeship in a hard school, but henceforward he never looked back, unless one can regard the Keynotes Series as a rather feeble revival of the Morte Darthur manner.

The article by Joseph Pennell, always a generous, though hot-headed, critic, in the first number of The Studio in April 1893, brought him a certain amount of réclame, but more important still it brought the contract to illustrate the English edition of Oscar Wilde's Salome published early in 1894. The play has had a succès de scandale, mainly over the question of representing John the Baptist in a public performance, and this has created a grievance and has obscured the merits, or rather demerits, of the play itself. But to the clear sighted Beardsley, it can be pretty well assumed, the poverty of the play was obvious from the start. Wilde himself, and the characters, are gently derided throughout his astonishing designs. Never had a book been so illustrated with such irrelevant and irreverent and irrational drawings. And never before had black and white been pushed to such an extreme of pattern and plan. Something of the eroticism of Rops, something of the charm of Japanese ladies of the Tea Gardens is apparent in these designs. But in the main they are just Beardsley—his wayward, perverse self.

The book is indeed a remarkable one, both for content and illustration, and it is no wonder that knowledgeable admirers of the artist will sometimes state it is his greatest work, a view I do not share. That it was a puzzle to the publisher, John Lane, as well as to the critics is shown by the number of designs that were discarded or altered, but that it established the artist and made him famous must be denied. A total of only 600 copies of the special and ordinary editions was printed, and contemporary reviews were few and far between. The big reviews mainly passed it by, as indeed they did the Morte Darthur. His world-wide reputation was to come later.

But these important drawings brought him valuable contacts with the writers who were then working for John Lane, and his illustrations were of such originality that they could not be ignored. Indeed, this work has been more often reprinted than any other book of Wilde, and probably more for the drawings than the text.

His next venture, in April 1894, a few months after the publication of Salome, was to bring him that universal approval and opprobrium, which caused Punch to publish a full-page caricature of Britannia à la Beardsley in its Almanack for 1895, and Punch had an unerring touch for what was "on the town" at the moment.

At least ten gentlemen have claimed to be the originators of The Yellow Book. At this distance of time it is impossible to tell who is the rightful claimant, but at least Beardsley was in it from the very beginning as Art Editor.

The boom years of 1893-4 produced many periodicals, most of them to disappear in a few months, but The Yellow Book was to be different: it was to be a quarterly and bound and the covers were to be a flaunting yellow. In fact, it was to be a challenge to the vested interests in art and literature, as the New English Art Club was in the realm of painting.

There is no doubt that the first four numbers were a phenomenal success. It was widely advertised, much criticized and rapidly bought. Several editions were published, an unusual thing in periodical literature. Both text and illustrations received violent praise and blame from the Left and Right Wings respectively. The artist, for about a year, was notorious and was fêted and flattered.

This adulation might have been disastrous to the work of a young man just out of his teens, but there is no doubt his cool, detached sanity saved him from being the pet of the drawing-rooms of the rich, the influential and the arty. For this year he gave the world of his very best. John Lane was an astute publisher, he realized that *les jeunes* had got the bit between their teeth and he wisely gave them a loose rein. Until the Wilde trial came as a thunderbolt, there were no squabbles in The Bodley Head. In every number Beardsley produced some startling, mordant, bitter or freshly beautiful design. The covers alone were enough to arrest the man in the street, as they were meant to do, with their thick black lines on bright yellow, the colour of the daring French novel. Such drawings as as L'Education Sentimentale, a Night Piece and Mrs. Patrick Campbell made the academical foam at the mouth. A well-known review suggested that a short act of Parliament should be passed to "stop this sort of thing". How right they seemed! As a fact, in a few short months, an act of Parliament brought Oscar Wilde to the artistic gallows, and with him the Nineties as we understand the phrase today. But what never dies is the artistic urge, and Beardsley, ill and dying, was yet to do his greatest work. In the second number appeared the wonderfully observed Garçons de Café and the supreme outline drawing of Madame Réjane. This drawing, bought originally for a £5 note which the artist immediately lost, was finally acquired by Vienna in the days when she was still a leading light in artistic Europe.

For the third volume Beardsley prepared a little plot for the critics in the

Whistler tradition. He published two drawings under the names of Philip Broughton and Albert Foschter. The critics fell to a man, not one of them recognised the real artist, one even writing of "his well-known style". None of them, needless to say, had a good word for two of his finest satires, Lady Gold's Escort and the famous Wagnerites. It will be noticed that both these are executed in pure chiaroscuro, and no half lights are attempted, yet the outer night seen from the blazing entrance to the Lyceum, and the curious glare from the footlights in Covent Garden are perfectly rendered. Nothing comparable to this had been attempted in Western art hitherto. The Wagnerites in the original is marred by the use of Chinese white, but it may probably be the work of the block maker, who was often a bungler in the far-off Nineties.

In the fourth volume of The Yellow Book, the last in which his work appeared, he published The Mysterious Rose Garden, in which for almost the first time he abandons the earlier conventions for hair, and gives us those exquisite wavy lines which must have been the despair of block-makers and overlay cutters. It is again in pure black and white, yet how wonderfully is suggested the upward light on the roses from the lantern. One can imagine the feelings of "respectable folk" when it was mooted that this was Beardsley's idea of The Annunciation! In the same volume appeared The Repentance of Mrs. . . . , and the Frontispiece for Juvenal which was skitted by Punch. The former is a new drawing of the same subject as The Litany of Mary Magdalen drawn in 1892 and a comparison of them will show the astonishing advance in his work in two years. The latter has a brilliant architectural background, suggesting the once gracious beauty of Portland Place, the Adelphi, Shepherd's Market, Regent Street and other gems of eighteenth century and Regency architecture, now lost to us for ever. Here again Beardsley was before his time.

Throughout 1894 he had been far from idle. Contemporary with his work for The Yellow Book he had been making cover designs, for which he had a genius, frontispieces, title pages, end papers and posters for John Lane and other publishers. In fact, the demand for his work was incessant. Good health and good spirits went hand in hand, and with his social demands it was extraordinary how much work he accomplished.

The fourth volume was published in January 1895, but by the time the April number was due to appear, Oscar Wilde was being tried, retried and sentenced under the Criminal Law Amendment Act. "This sort of thing" had, indeed, found its short act of Parliament. Henceforward the aesthetic, fin de siècle Nineties were under a cloud for many a year.

The injustice of all this to Beardsley was patent. Not only had he not associated with Wilde since Salome, but Wilde had never contributed to The Yellow Book, the firm of Lane was not his only publisher, and Beardsley's appetites were never called in question as being other than normal.

But the scandal was too great. Beardsley had to suffer with many another innocent. Actually many a well-known figure in Society (some unlikely ones, too) suddenly found that Spring on the Continent was more charming than in this country.

John Lane at the time was in America, he received an ultimatum by telegram from one of his more important writers and bowed to the storm. Beardsley had to go.

The fifth volume was ready for press, his illustrations printed, but the whole edition was scrapped, and thereafter The Yellow Book became dull and lifeless. These drawings were subsequently published elsewhere, though they were announced in the prospectus for the fifth volume.

Beardsley had left 114 Cambridge Street, where most of The Yellow Book work was done and had taken a lease of 57 Chester Terrace. This he surrendered in December 1895, and thereafter was to become a wanderer.

Some time in the summer of 1895 he became associated with Leonard Smithers, about whom I have written elsewhere. This connection was to last until his death, and all his future work was published by Smithers. It was to be his best.

Major Haldane Macfall, unfortunately with much verbiage and circumlocution, has pointed out the important fact that Beardsley altered his style almost yearly in the five years of his working life. But the year was not the calendar one, and the change usually took place in the summer. His work must therefore be divided into the years 1892-3, 1893-4, etc. And with this change came also a change in his signature.

The summer of 1895, in spite of the serious set-back of his dismissal from The Yellow Book, was no exception. The Prospectus for Vol. 5 shows us what drawings would have been published. They include Atalanta (without hound) and A Chopin Nocturne. The last is wholly in wash and line and the former has wash in the foreground. The Nocturne is, of course, a companion to the supreme Chopin Ballade III. Here then is a definite break from his Yellow Book technique, and a foretaste of the later Mademoiselle de Maupin set. Both the Chopin drawings are in sepia and both show a mastery of this medium. It is probable that the Ballade was going to be published in The Studio as it was owned by Charles Holme, who did not issue it until after the artist's death. Smithers made unsuccessful attempts to obtain it for the Book of Fifty Drawings, and when it was published in The Studio in May 1898, it was very badly reproduced.

The Chopin Ballade is one of the greatest works of this artist. Not only does it seem to interpret the exquisite piano music of another genius, so that persons wholly blind to Beardsley's line are charmed with it, but the values are masterly. It is done in five flat washes, arranged with infinite subtlety, and with all the economy of an early Japanese woodcut in colours.

The early correspondence with Smithers shows that they were both groping for new matter, and The Queen in Exile is considered; this became Under the Hill. Next we see from these letters that a very happy choice is made, probably at the suggestion of Edmund Gosse, and he is working gaily at The Rape of the Lock, in many ways his greatest, and certainly his most popular, set of drawings.

Before the end of the year 1895, both publisher and artist had decided to issue The Savoy, and so it came about that the drawing of The Rape of the Lock first appeared in No. 2 for April 1896. These drawings show a verve, a wit and appreciation of the poem that can scarcely be matched in English illustration. One can as easily imagine Alice in Wonderland without Tenniel as this poem without Beardsley's drawings. It is said that Pope undertook the work to heal, not to widen, the breach between two families, caused by the familiarity of a gentleman in cutting off a tress of Miss Fermor's locks. The drawings therefore are poised on that subtle satiric edge where one laughs, but does not sneer. There is a charm, an *insouciance* a seeming naivety, unknown in any other of his illustrations. One feels he was as happy in making them as Pope was in writing the poem. Indeed at this time he is full of spirits, and the year 1895-6 saw a prodigious number of fine works.

It is probable that with the approach of each summer his lungs became better and he once more had hopes, which were each autumn to be dashed to the ground. But by the end of 1896 it was obvious, even to himself, that he had not long to live.

With the publication of The Savoy, printed on rather cheap spongy paper, Beardsley had to return to pen and ink though he was later to resort to wash.

The Rape of the Lock heralds this great period. His art had reached absolute maturity and it was now merely a question how far his tuberculosis would permit him to work; only a bad haemorrhage could hold him back. However, the haemorrhages *were* bad, so much so that the sixth number of the Savoy only contained one new drawing, The Fourth Tableau of Das Rheingold, and it was decided to close the magazine with the eighth issue.

However, the year 1896 was a fertile one, for besides The Rape of the Lock he made in the summer the eight drawings for The Lysistrata, and he and Smithers were preparing the Book of Fifty Drawings for press.

The Lysistrata are in their own way as great an achievement as The Rape. Unfortunately most are too free for ordinary publication and the text of the play by Aristophanes is equally Rabelaisian. They constitute another change, being executed in line without shading, recession or background. It will therefore be realized that this line must suggest modelling, and, in fact, they have a sculpturesque beauty seldom matched in his other work. Such drawings as Ave atque Vale and the Frontispiece to The Comedy of the Rhinegold really suggest all the subtle planes of the human torso with but two lines.

Towards the end of the year 1896 he was doing the Pierrot of the Minute series for Dowson's play. The cover is unusually brilliant even for him and the Frontispiece almost rivals the Rape drawings again.

For the eighth number of The Savoy it is clear everything was got together to make a last good showing. Four of the drawings had been intended for some version of Wagner's Rheingold, probably to be written in prose by Beardsley himself. At this time it is pathetic to see in his letters how after every bad attack of haemorrhage his spirits revive and, like all consumptives, he begins to be optimistic and to entertain extravagant notions of the amount of work he will do. Within a few months of his death he proposed to make 24 drawings for Volpone, for which, in fact, he only made seven. An example of his optimism is the design for the cover of Volpone which is dated Paris 1898. But he had been obliged to leave Paris for Mentone in November 1897 and he writes that ''the journey nearly did for me''.

He returned to the use of sepia in the Spring of 1897 with the six designs for Mademoiselle de Maupin, and these were published posthumously, as was Volpone. These are wonderfully delicate, but one feels somehow a flagging of the strength and vigour of his last Savoy work. They are quite inconsequential and, in fact, it is doubtful if they were all intended for the book. But these and the Volpone Initials show that he was again changing his style if not his medium. The latter are in pencil with a pen outline and are as elaborate and rich as the Savoy work is clear and simple. The Volpone Frontispiece was intended only for the Prospectus. Some critics have seen in these five Initials a new departure and the beginning of a return to nature, but as a fact the letter written in December 1897, giving a list of the 24 drawings, only shows one of them to be in wash. It is uncertain therefore, had he lived, how his art would have shaped. On the one hand the illustrations might have become rivals to The Rape, for Ben Jonson was much to his liking, and on the other they might have been as diffuse as the Mademoiselle de Maupin, with little of grip on his subject.

It is only right and wise to suspend judgment on these last pencil drawings. Right because he had been a dying man from the summer of 1897, and wise because his powers of recuperation were amazing. No one in April 1895 could have foreseen the brilliant sequence of drawings he produced in The Rape of the Lock and The Savoy, and this when his disease was gaining on him relentlessly.

With that pathetic ''if'' that goes with consumption, if the climate of Mentone had suited him, if the winter had been drier, if he had gone to Egypt or South Africa or Madeira, if he had only gone to Grasse or Switzerland, he might have completed another series for Ben Jonson's play as great as those for Pope's satire.

But as Arthur Symons has so truly written, ''Beardsley ended a long career at the age of twenty-six'', and as we pass the end of a half century since his death, we are fortunate in being more able to understand his genius than were his contemporaries.

The Nineties are really a long time ago. When Beardsley was working two World Wars had not been fought and the South African War had not even begun. When he was publishing his shocking Yellow Book drawings, British complacency had not been shaken since the Crimea. The streets of London were mainly of macadam and were full of horse-drawn vehicles; gas lamps flared, crossing-sweepers were numerous and golden half-sovereigns slipped through one's fingers—or through holes in one's pockets. Ladies did not dine in restaurants, unless to meet their lovers in private rooms. Girls at dances were dutifully returned to their chaperones after every dance, and married women to their husbands. Out of doors, women had to give one hand to the holding of their skirts which would otherwise sweep the ground, while the other was for a parasol or the arm of a gentleman. They were always veiled and gloved. The veil was lifted as far as the nose to allow the partaking of tea when on a call and the gloves were skin tight and had to be put on with powder blown into them. Deportment was the thing, and a mother corrected her schoolgirl daughter if she crossed her legs when seated. Only ankles were for public view.

And so the horrific content of his drawings came upon the staid Victorian with a cold shock a younger generation simply cannot imagine. Today a Camden Town Murder by Sickert leaves us still cool and collected, and passages in novels which in those days would have brought about a prosecution are not even commented on in reviews.

Today, with so many art isms and ists, our blood pressure remains normal when we gaze at a series of coloured blots catalogued as The Immaculate Conception, or some fine ruled lines on an otherwise bare canvas called Bank Holiday 4 p.m. Any young art student of eighteen finding an old Yellow Book in a bookshop would wonder what all the pother was about.

So now we can appreciate all the easier the supreme craftsmanship of Beardsley without being alarmed at the subjects he depicts. In his day it was the extreme chastity of his line coupled with the then unchastity of the content that caused the public to gasp as from an ice-cold shower.

Actually the power of line as compared with tone, mass and colour is no new thing in England. It can be traced back to the time when English miniaturists were supreme, even to Anglo-Saxon and Celtic art. Miniatures as early as the twelfth century are easily identified by experts as English by these same strong, linear and even glyptic qualities that Beardsley possessed in such a marked degree. And it can be safely said that he was quite ignorant of Early English art, his tastes lying in the Renaissance and in Rococo.

Beardsley's literary efforts have so far not been touched on. It must be said at once that they are good amateur, but only amateur work. Had he received a hard grounding, say, in Fleet Street, as he had with the Morte Darthur, he might have become equally proficient in letters. None the less they cannot be ignored, more especially as they have self-inspired him to make some of his greatest drawings. Probably the best is an English translation of Carmen CI of Catullus:

By ways remote and distant waters sped,
Brother, to thy sad grave-side am I come,

That I may give the last gifts to the dead,
    And vainly parley with thin ashes dumb:
Since she who now bestows and now denies
    Has ta'en thee, hapless brother, from mine eyes.

But lo! these gifts, the heirlooms of past years,
    Are made sad things to grace thy coffin shell,
Take them, all drench'd with a brother's tears,
    And, brother, for all time, hail and farewell!

For this he made the moving Ave atque Vale, a truly classic masterpiece, with none of the sneer and satire which mars his work for many. It is allied to an earlier drawing, The Death of Pierrot, for which he wrote this strangely haunting caption, "As the dawn broke, Pierrot fell into his last sleep. Then upon tiptoe, silently up the stair, noiselessly into the room, came the comedians Arlecchino, Pantaleone, il Dottore, and Columbina, who with much love carried away upon their shoulders, the white frocked clown of Bergamo; whither we know not."

This quotation alone is proof that he could write. How perfectly, in prose and in line, is rendered the passing of the Comedia dell'Arte, how perfectly it presages his own!

In No. 3 of The Savoy he published The Ballad of a Barber, a suavely sinister poem, that is well known and often quoted. Again for this he executed a magnificent design, The Coiffing. Though he did many lovely toilet scenes, this is possibly the finest. The values are impeccable, as witness the contrasted thick, stiff satin ribbons and the delicate muslin peignoir of the Princess. It is subtly pyramidical, starting with the footstool at the base and climbing to the pointed tiara on the head of a figure of the Virgin on a Victorian chest. Truly the Princess is "as lyrical and sweet as one of Schubert's melodies".

In the first two issues of The Savoy appeared Under the Hill, the title changed from The Queen in Exile and this again altered from Venus and Tannhauser which John Lane had announced. The text of the latter differs much from Under the Hill, and was published privately by Smithers in an unexpurgated form.

The fragment in The Savoy (and indeed the "romantic Novel" was never finished) again calls forth some splendid illustrations, including the truly great Third Tableau of Das Rheingold and The Ascension of St Rose of Lima, neither having really much to do with the story. The Third Tableau has an Eastern rhythm and flow unsurpassed in the West either then or since. Nothing can rival it but the early Buddhist paintings in China, many of which were then undiscovered. The wonderful flame-like Loge is however entirely original, and it cannot be suggested, without evidence at present not forthcoming, that Beardsley had any contacts with early Chinese art. It must be regarded, as I have said, as *hors concours*. St Rose of Lima again has that flowing, swinging line, but it is plainly inspired by Durer's Great Fortune.

Although described as romantic, Under the Hill is more an essay in Rococo. It is purposely artificial, and some of the writer's effects hardly come off today. But it gives us an insight into Beardsley's teeming and fevered brain. There are many extraordinary descriptions of costume, and if the pencil and the pen had been denied him, he might have become a dress designer of note in the days when ladies were not afraid to pile effect on effect and hats carried fur, feather and textile all together. I have spoken elsewhere of Beardsley as a designer of costume, but it may be remarked how original are some of the dresses in his drawings. The right-hand figure of the titlepage of The Savoy No. 1 was once carried out as a design, in black, green and white for a Slade School fancy dress dance, complete with a three-foot fan, and won much praise.

Beardsley also published in The Savoy a poem of The Three Musicians, but this does not compare favourably to The Ballad of a Barber. He also wrote a short but cogent article on the Poster.

His own posters were all successful, the best being for the Avenue Theatre, where a short season of three plays was given. This Poster, printed in blue and green, must have been voted, in 1894, as bizarre and outré as the three plays given, A Comedy of Sighs by Dr John Todhunter, Arms and the Man by G. B. Shaw and The Land of Heart's Desire by W. B. Yeats. All three were unsuccessful and only one has survived as drama today. But the poster itself can be regarded as a landmark in striking design and vivid colour rivalling those of the Beggarstaff Brothers.

Finally one might summarize by saying that the art of Beardsley is esoteric, while he himself is eclectic. He ranged far and wide, both in French and in English literature. Having found a subject, he made it peculiarly his own. His illustrations are entirely wayward and of his own choosing. He was never under bondage to the writer, as were artists from Dickens to Trollope. Indeed, in Salome he guyed the author! He never spoke or wrote of making illustrations to a book, but rather of "making pictures for a book". Even in a posthumous work, Volpone, his work is described as "illustrative and decorative": the Morte Darthur is "embellished", Salome is "pictured" and The Rape is "embroidered". The significance of these words is plain. They were not chosen haphazard by the publisher, they were dictated by Beardsley himself. When the last Morte Darthur drawing was finished he never again became a hack.

His work is a commentary on the text, rather as his Yellow Book drawings were a commentary on the life around him. What particular part of life he registered with his skilful pen was his own affair. To have done otherwise would have been a betrayal of all the ground won by the New English Art Club, of which he was a member, and by Whistler in a generation of fights with the critics.

Beardsley's art is for the most part two dimensional, if not planographic. There is seldom any depth in his compositions. And as much as possible, there are no high lights and no shadows. The blockmaker is blamed for the shadow on the neck of the Virgin in A Christmas Card, but we doubt if he was at fault. In The Three Musicians the light can come only from the clearing in the wood, yet the figures are equally illuminated. In two of the Rape of the Lock drawings we face the light from the windows, yet again there are no shadows. In the Baron's Prayer and The Toilet, from the same set, wall and floor are on the same plane. He adopts the Eastern convention in which there is no angle of light. It has been said that a Chinese artist was puzzled by finding that all the sitters to Western painters had part of their faces clean and part dirty. When he was told that, as the light came from one quarter only, the side of the face not subject to this light was in shadow, he was left marvelling at the strange conventions of Western mankind. The concern of Beardsley was not to create an illusion of reality, but, like the Eastern artist, to make a beautiful design or pattern within a given space.

In character he was friendly and lovable, though witty and daring. He made many friends, though few enemies. There was but little rancour or bitterness in his make-up, though there was a streak of waywardness and perversity which he probably inherited from his mother. A medical friend has also pointed out that he may have inherited his uncanny ability to diagnose character from his maternal grandfather and great-grandfather who were both physicians and surgeons.

He took his art with all the seriousness which is its due, and he often speaks with affection of a drawing that has just left his hands, or is on the point of completion. They were, indeed, his children.

His eroticism is manifest, and must be accepted as simply as the fact that he had auburn hair and long hands. Much of it was due to his tuberculosis, with which it is often associated, and also to frustration due to that illness and the retired life he had to lead after 1895, and indeed earlier. For him it was from drawing-table, to sofa, to bed. Even a carriage to an evening concert was taken in great trepidation. How many of his drawings are of interiors, or conceived in formal gardens. How few of them are set in the country, and this country is more derived from Claude than from the English landscape. And yet it is pathetic to read in his letters that he is having "a spell of warm weather, troubled only by the wasps, that bring however with them a sort of memory of orchards", and again that "jolly winds are driving white clouds over the bluest sky".

Having mastered his medium he pushed it to the farthest degree, in fact as far as it had ever been taken or is likely to be. In this he resembles Meryon in his Eauxfortes sur Paris, or Rembrandt in his landscapes, or Rowlandson's tinted drawings. He is as much a master of pen and ink as Goya was of aquatint, or Handel was of the combination of voice and trumpet.

To this consummate skill was added an imagination hitherto unknown and undreamt of in the staid, prosperous and smug later nineteenth century. Demon ridden it may be, but we have to go back to Heironymus Bosch to find anything comparable. And he has a delicacy and refinement unknown to the Flemish painter. Over a blank white paper come a smirking, creeping, posturing devil horde of things, grotesque, weird, macabre, sinister, misgiving and alarming, before which the creatures in Comus and The End of Elphintown retreat abashed. And then with a seeming flick of his faery hand, we see only a harmless fop of George I, a charming little lady at her toilet, or a poor dead doll.

If Art is to make us wonder and ponder, to revere and appreciate, if it is not merely to serve us with the surface prettiness of things, then surely the art of Aubrey Vincent Beardsley can be ranged beside that of the Great Ones.

June 1948

The following selected English bibliography contains biographical matter and criticisms of the art of Aubrey Beardsley:

BEERBOHM, MAX. Tomorrow, January 1897. The Idler, May 1898.

BURDETT, OSBERT. The Beardsley Period. 1925. John Lane.

DICTIONARY OF NATIONAL BIOGRAPHY.

GRAY, JOHN. The Last Letters of Aubrey Beardsley. 1904. Longmans.

HARLAND, HENRY. The Academy. 10 December 1898.

HIND, C. LEWIS. (Introduction by) The Uncollected Work of Aubrey Beardsley. 1925. John Lane.

JACKSON, HOLBROOK. The Eighteen Nineties. 1913. Grant Richards.

LAWRENCE, ARTHUR H. The Idler, March 1897.

MACFALL, HALDANE. Aubrey Beardsley. 1927. Simon & Schuster. New York.

MARILLIER, H. C. (Preface by) The Early and Later Work of Aubrey Beardsley. 2 Vols. 1899 and 1901. John Lane.

MURDOCH, W. G. BLAIKIE. The Renaissance of the Nineties. 1911. De La More Press.

ROSS, ROBERT. Aubrey Beardsley. 1909. John Lane.

SYMONS, ARTHUR. Aubrey Beardsley. 1898. Unicorn Press and 1905, Dent.

WALKER, R. A. (Editor) An Aubrey Beardsley Lecture by A. W. King. 1924. R. A. Walker.

WALKER, R. A. (Editor) The Letters of Aubrey Beardsley to Leonard Smithers. 1937. First Edition Club.

THE BEST OF BEARDSLEY

1. The Kiss of Judas. From the Pall Mall Magazine, July 1893. One of two drawings he made for this periodical.

THE KISS OF
JUDAS

2. The Woman in the Moon, 1893. From Salome by Oscar Wilde. John Lane, 1894. The drawing has little connection with the play. A caricature of Wilde in the moon.

3. The Peacock Skirt. 1893. From Salome by Oscar Wilde. John Lane, 1894. A drawing strongly influenced by the Japanese print through Whistler's Peacock Room.

4. The Black Cape. 1893. From Salome by Oscar Wilde. John Lane, 1894.
The drawing has no connection with the play and is a caricature of the fashion
of the period.

8. The Eyes of Herod. 1893. From Salome by Oscar Wilde. John Lane, 1894. Another drawing influenced by Whistler's Peacock Room, and with a Butterfly in the top left corner. Wilde is again caricatured.

9. The Stomach Dance. 1893. From Salome by Oscar Wilde. John Lane, 1894. The lower figure is reminiscent of the Bon-Mots grotesques.

10. The Toilette of Salome. I. 1893. Intended for Salome, but suppressed. The first of many toilet scenes he drew.

11. The Toilette of Salome. II. 1893. From Salome by Oscar Wilde. John Lane, 1894. The drawing substituted for the previous one.

12. The Dancer's Reward. 1893. From Salome by Oscar Wilde. John Lane, 1894. The drawing of the hands is not as successful as usual.

13. The Climax. 1893. From Salome by Oscar Wilde. John Lane, 1894. A version of the drawing J'ai baisé ta Bouche which first appeared in The Studio No. 1, for April 1893. It was probably that drawing which procured him the commission to illustrate Salome.

14. Tailpiece. 1893. From Salome by Oscar Wilde. John Lane, 1894.

15. Salome on Settle. 1893. Intended for the book but suppressed. It is also called Maîtresse d'Orchestre. It resembles a Bon-Mots grotesque.

16. Frontispiece to Plays by John Davidson. 1893. John Lane, 1894. This contains caricatures of Augustus Harris, Wilde, Genée, Mabel Beardsley and Richard Le Gallienne.

17. Cover Design for The Yellow Book, Vol. I, 1894.   John Lane.   A splendid design in the Chéret manner. Printed in black on bright yellow cloth.

18. L'Education Sentimentale. 1894. From The Yellow Book Vol. I. This drawing created much stir at the time. The left-hand figure, reproduced here, was subsequently cut off and tinted by the artist and renamed Mrs Marsuple (from Under the Hill). The right-hand figure is probably destroyed.

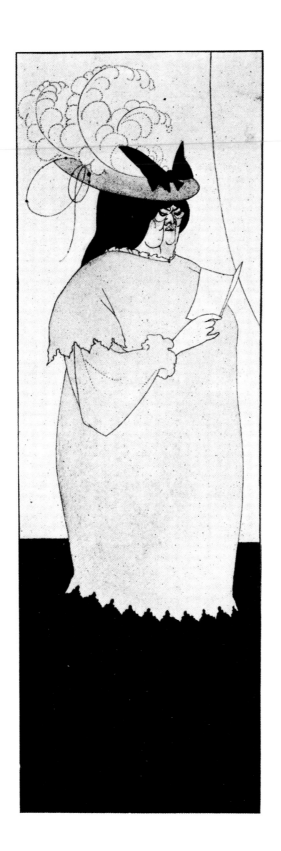

19. Les Passades. 1894. From the Winter Number of Today. It is a companion drawing to Night Piece in Vol. I of The Yellow Book. Though carried out in pure black and white, with no half-tone, it is wonderfully atmospheric.

20. Mrs Patrick Campbell. 1894. From The Yellow Book, Vol. I. This harmless, but clever, caricature was greeted with a howl of execration at the time. The subject was the idol of the Gallery in The Second Mrs. Tanqueray.

21. Cover Design for The Yellow Book, Vol. II. 1894. Another bold and effective design.

22. Comedy-Ballet of Marionettes I. 1894. From The Yellow Book, Vol. II. The artist's only painting in oils is a version of this drawing, now in the Tate Gallery and known as A Caprice.

23. Comedy-Ballet of Marionettes II. 1894. From The Yellow Book, Vol. II. Note the decorative value of the laced-up back.

24. Comedy-Ballet of Marionettes III. 1894. From The Yellow Book, Vol. I. The central female figure was cut out and renamed The Black Domino, and was in the collection of the late Judge Evans. It was also named Dancer with the Domino and exhibited at the International Society's Exhibition of Fair Women, 1909.

25. Garçons de Café. 1894. From The Yellow Book, Vol. II. The original was once the property of the artist's House-Master at the Brighton Grammar School and is believed to have been destroyed.

26. Madame Réjane. 1894. From The Yellow Book, Vol. II
The best of the artist's many drawings of the great French actress
whom he knew personally, indeed, one of his finest works. The
figure is perfectly posed and full of life. He sold it to the late
Fredk. H. Evans for a £5 note, put this in his outside pocket and
lost it in half an hour.

27. Cover Design for The Yellow Book, Vol. III. 1894. The conceit of using two street lamps for the lighting of a lady's toilet mirror was the sort of anomaly that puzzled and irritated the critics of the period.

28. Portrait of Himself. 1894. From The Yellow Book, Vol. III
Compared to the pomposities in the Uffizi Gallery, this is a
delightfully witty self-portrait. It has a gorgeous air of
sumptuousness though carried out with extreme economy of line.

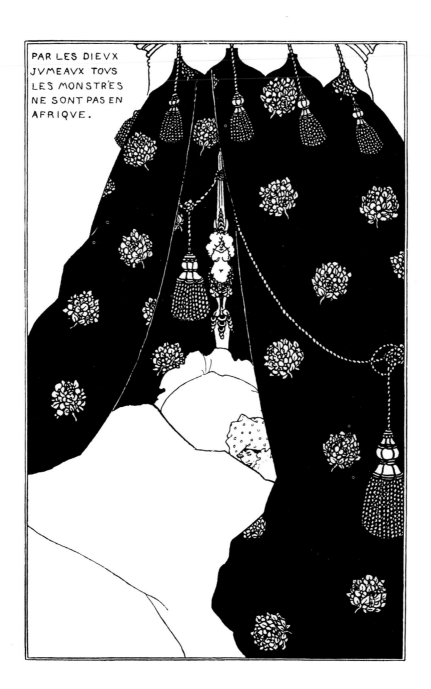

29. Lady Gold's Escort. 1894. From The Yellow Book, Vol. III
A social satire which was not graciously received by the critics
of the day. Though in pure black and white, light and shadow are
brilliantly suggested.

30. The Wagnerites. 1894. From The Yellow Book, Vol. III. One of the most admired drawings of this period. We again get an illusion of shadow with no shading used. The original is one of the few in which Chinese white is used, but this may have been put on by the block-maker.

31. La Dame aux Camélias. 1894. From The Yellow Book, Vol.III
The drawing was later tinted in colour. It was also reproduced in a
larger size than that used for the magazine.

32. Cover Design for The Yellow Book, Vol. IV. 1894. This was the last cover design by the artist to be used for the magazine.

33. The Mysterious Rose Garden. 1894. From The Yellow Book, Vol. IV. A mysteriously beautiful drawing. The bright light from the lantern is suggested without the use of shading. The earlier convention for hair has been abandoned in favour of a more realistic treatment.

34. The Repentance of Mrs . . . 1894. From **The Yellow Book**, Vol. IV.   A similar subject to The Litany of Mary Magdalen done in his earlier Burne-Jones manner in 1892. Vide Later Work of A.B., p. 7.

THE REPENTANCE
OF M^{RS} ....

35. Miss Winifred Emery. 1894. From The Yellow Book, Vol. IV
A theatrical portrait, but not so successful as that of Mrs. Patrick
Campbell.

36. Frontispiece for Juvenal. 1894. From The Yellow Book, Vol. IV. A skit of this drawing appeared in Punch. The background recalls the fact that the artist was for a short time in an architect's office.

37. Design for a Yellow Book Cover. 1894-5. This design was not used.

38. Madame Réjane (Half-length). 1894. A fine likeness of the famous actress in the part of Madame Sans Gêne.

42. A Suggested Reform in Ballet Costume. 1895. From A London Garland. Macmillan, 1895. An unfinished drawing once owned by the late Joseph Pennell. It is one of the earliest drawings to bear his full signature. It is also called At a Distance.

43. Singer Poster Design. 1895. First published in The Poster for October 1898. A rare poster, with the same subject, a woman playing a piano in the open, as that of the titlepage ornament in The Yellow Book, Vol. I. This called forth an amusing letter from the artist to The Pall Mall Budget, published in Under the Hill, 1904.

44. Frontispiece for Venus and Tannhauser. 1895. Not so used. The unfinished story was later published privately by Smithers without illustrations. It has also been called Venus between Terminal Gods. Note the statuesque simplicity of Venus against the elaborate and decorative background.

VENUS.

45. Frontispiece and Titlepage for Venus and Tannhauser. 1895. Not so used. Probably an alternate proposal for an illustrated edition of the story. The architectural border is only one drawing reversed. The background is still reminiscent of the Morte Darthur.

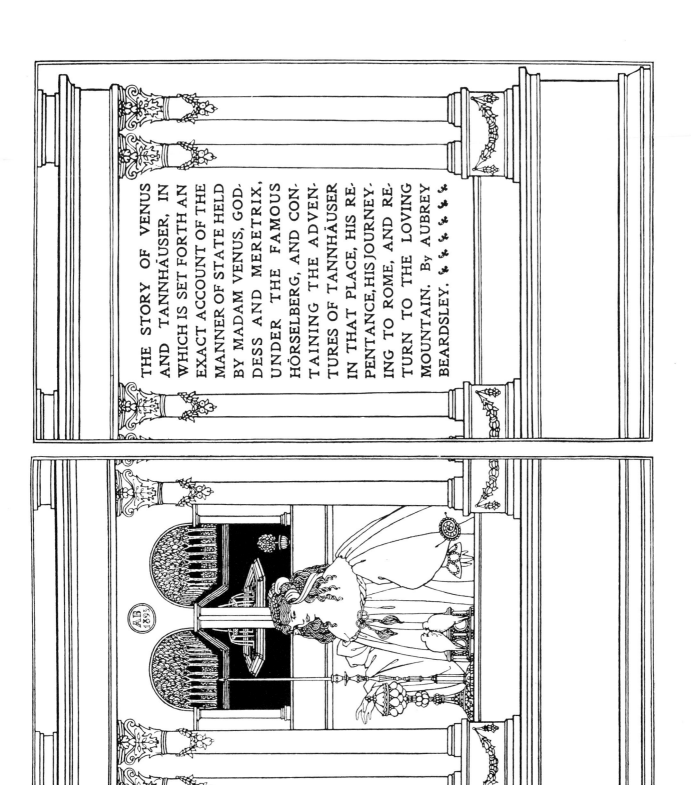

THE STORY OF VENUS AND TANNHÄUSER, IN WHICH IS SET FORTH AN EXACT ACCOUNT OF THE MANNER OF STATE HELD BY MADAM VENUS, GODDESS AND MERETRIX, UNDER THE FAMOUS HÖRSELBERG, AND CONTAINING THE ADVENTURES OF TANNHÄUSER IN THAT PLACE, HIS REPENTANCE, HIS JOURNEYING TO ROME, AND RETURN TO THE LOVING MOUNTAIN. By AUBREY BEARDSLEY.

46. The Return of Tannhäuser to the Venusberg. 1895. The same subject as an earlier drawing called Tannhäuser (Later Work of A.B., p. 70). A very dramatic effect is obtained by placing the hands against the black background.

47. Cover Design for Yellow Book Prospectus for Vol. V. 1895. Not used in Vol. V. He adapted this design for Smithers Catalogue of Rare Books.

48. Atalanta I. 1895. The earlier drawing (without hound) intended for The Yellow Book, Vol. V.

51. A Nocturne of Chopin. 1895. Executed like the previous drawing in flat sepia washes. He abandoned this medium for most of his work for Leonard Smithers, but reverted to it in the Mademoiselle de Maupin set.

52. Messalina. 1895. Probably intended as one of the illustrations to the Sixth Satire of Juvenal.

53. Frontispiece for Earl Lavender by John Davidson. 1895. Ward & Downey. Note the decorative value of the Victorian mantelpiece, fireplace and fender.

AUBREY
BEARDSLEY.

54. Isolde. 1895. First published in The Studio for October 1895, where it was reproduced by lithography in colours.

ISOLDE

55. Black Coffee. 1895. Originally intended for Vol. V of The Yellow Book but not used. Also intended for the frontispiece to An Evil Motherhood, but suppressed.

57. The Mirror of Love.   1895.   From Aubrey Beardsley by Arthur Symons, 1898.
Unicorn Press. The drawing was probably intended as a frontispiece to a book by André
Raffalovitch.

58. Cover Design to Sappho. 1895. Edited by H. T. Wharton. John Lane.
One of the many successful cover designs made by the artist.

59. The Dream. 1895-6. From the Rape of The Lock. Smithers, 1896. This and the succeeding nine drawings constitute, in the opinion of many, Beardsley's chef d'œuvre. They are all imbued with an Eighteenth Century sparkle and wit in perfect harmony with the poem. The amazing skill of the dotted line design on the bed-hangings has only to be attempted to be properly appreciated.

> Belinda still her downy pillow pressed,
> Her guardian sylph prolonged the balmy rest:
> 'Twas he had summoned to her silent bed
> The morning dream that hovered o'er her head.

60. The Billet-Doux. 1895-6. From The Rape of the Lock. Smithers, 1896. One of the most delightful epitomes of the feminine the artist has made.

> 'Twas then, Belinda, if report say true,
> Thy eyes first opened on a billet-doux;

61. The Toilet. 1895-6. From The Rape of the Lock. Smithers, 1896.
One of the artist's many brilliant toilet scenes. Note the colourful
effect of rich brocades and velvets rendered merely in black and white.
And now, unveiled, the toilet stands displayed,
Each silver vase in mystic order laid.

62. The Baron's Prayer. 1895-6. From The Rape of the Lock. Smithers, 1896.
A supremely competent drawing though there is no third dimension.
The contrast of the rococo table and the wall decoration is remarkable.

      —to Love an altar built,
        Of twelve vast French romances, neatly gilt.
        There lay three garters, half a pair of gloves,
        And all the trophies of his former loves;

64. The Rape of the Lock. 1895-6. From The Rape of the Lock. Smithers, 1896. Although the spectator faces the light the figures are all equally illuminated. Possibly the first drawing he made for the set.

> He takes the gift with rev'rence, and extends
> The little engine on his fingers' ends;
> This just behind Belinda's neck he spread,
> As o'er the fragrant steams she bends her head.

65. The Cave of Spleen. 1895-6. From The Rape of the Lock. Smithers, 1896.
A phantasmagoria of the Rococo, and perhaps too crowded and tightly drawn.

> Umbriel, a dusky, melancholy sprite,
> As ever sullied the fair face of light,
> Down to the central earth, his proper scene
> Repaired to search the gloomy cave of Spleen.

67. The New Star. 1895-6. From The Rape of the Lock. Smithers, 1896. A perfect cul-de-lampe.
A sudden star, it shot through liquid air,
And drew behind a radiant trail of hair.

AB.

68. Cover Design. 1895-6. From The Rape of the Lock. Smithers, 1896. A very rich design carried out in gold on vellum in the limited edition.

69. Design for the Prospectus of The Savoy, I. 1895. This splendid caricature of John Bull was suppressed and the following was substituted.

70. Design for the Prospectus of The Savoy, II. 1895.
This design was used to replace the previous one.

PROSPECTUS
NUMBER
I
DEC 1st 1895

AVBREY BEARDSLEY.

71. Cover Design for The Savoy No. 1, 1895. As originally drawn the amour is making free with a copy of The Yellow Book at his feet, a reference to his parting with John Lane, but this was later altered.

THE SAVOY

AUBREY BEARDSLEY. 1896.

72. Titlepage to The Savoy Nos. 1 and 2. 1895. An example of Beardsley's amazing facility in designing costume.

73. Contents Page of The Savoy No. 1. 1895. A bolder
and better version of the Prospectus Design I above.

74. The Three Musicians. 1895. From The Savoy No. 1. An illustration to his Poem of this name. Note the absence of all chiaroscuro.

75. The Three Musicians. II. 1895. This
illustration was omitted from The Savoy No. 1.

76. The Bathers. 1895. From The Savoy No. 1. Also called On Dieppe Beach. It illustrates Arthur Symons's article on Dieppe.

77. Moska.   1895.   From The Savoy No. 1.
Another illustration to Symons's article on Dieppe.

MOSKA

78. The Abbé. 1895. From The Savoy No. 1.   The Abbé Fanfreluche in Beardsley's story Under the Hill. One of his most elaborate designs.

80. The Fruit Bearers. 1895. From The Savoy No. 1. Another illustration to Under the Hill. A compromise between pure black and white, and tone; possibly too elaborate.

81. A large Christmas Card. 1895. From The Savoy No. 1. Inserted loose with the first number of the magazine. His only religious drawing. He was not satisfied with the reproduction and it is one very hard to reproduce in line.

83. A Footnote. 1896. From The Savoy No. 2. A self portrait in which the artist has fatefully bound himself to the god of Nature.

84. The Ascension of St Rose of Lima. 1896. From The Savoy No. 2. A truly magnificent drawing full of grace and dignity and balance. It has the same power as Durer's Great Fortune.

85. The Third Tableau of Das Rheingold. 1896. From The Savoy No. 2. One of Beardsley's most splendid designs, showing an Eastern rhythm in the line and a unique imagination. He was a great admirer of Wagner's Ring and he here depicts Wotan, Loge and Fafner.

86. Cover Design for Savoy No. 3. 1896. Beardsley was always better at drawing a formal garden than a landscape.

AUBREY BEARDSLEY, ETC.

87. Titlepage Design for The Savoy No. 3. 1896. This happy drawing was afterwards adopted by Smithers as one of his trade marks and reproduced much smaller on covers of books. It is also known as Puck on Pegasus.

THE
SAVOY

88. The Coiffing. From The Savoy No. 3. 1896. To illustrate his poem The Ballad of a Barber. One of his greatest drawings and possibly the finest of his many toilet scenes. Note the subtle values of the French window, the dotted lines of the peignoir of the Princess and the thick lines of the ribbons; also the diagonal line rising from the footstool to the top of the Crown on the Virgin's head. Even the Victorian flower vase on the left adds to the decorative value.

AUBREY BEARDSLEY.

89. Cover Design for The Savoy No. 4. 1896. The curtain on the right is reminiscent of The Avenue Theatre Poster.

AUBREY BEARDSLEY.

90. Cover Design for The Savoy No. 5. 1896. At this time the artist was almost incapacitated by illness. It is somewhat reminiscent of the "still argent lake" in his story Under the Hill.

91. The Fourth Tableau of Das Rheingold. From The Savoy No. 6, 1896. Used as the cover design for this number. Another drawing of amazing imagination, representing Wotan and Loge, though not as fine as The Third Tableau. Illness prevented him from completing his series of drawings for The Rheingold.

92. The Death of Pierrot. From The Savoy No. 6. 1896. A beautiful and pathetic drawing which prophesied his approaching end.

94. Ave atque Vale.   From The Savoy No. 7.   1896.   A very beautiful drawing to illustrate Beardsley's translation of Carmen CI of Catullus.

95. Tristan und Isolde.   From The Savoy No. 7. 1896.
A later version of an earlier drawing. Beardsley made many
drawings for this great tragic opera of Wagner.

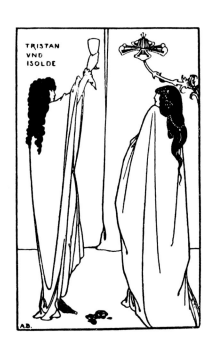

96. Cover Design for The Savoy No. 8. 1896. The drawing was also printed in colours and used as a showcard by Smithers.

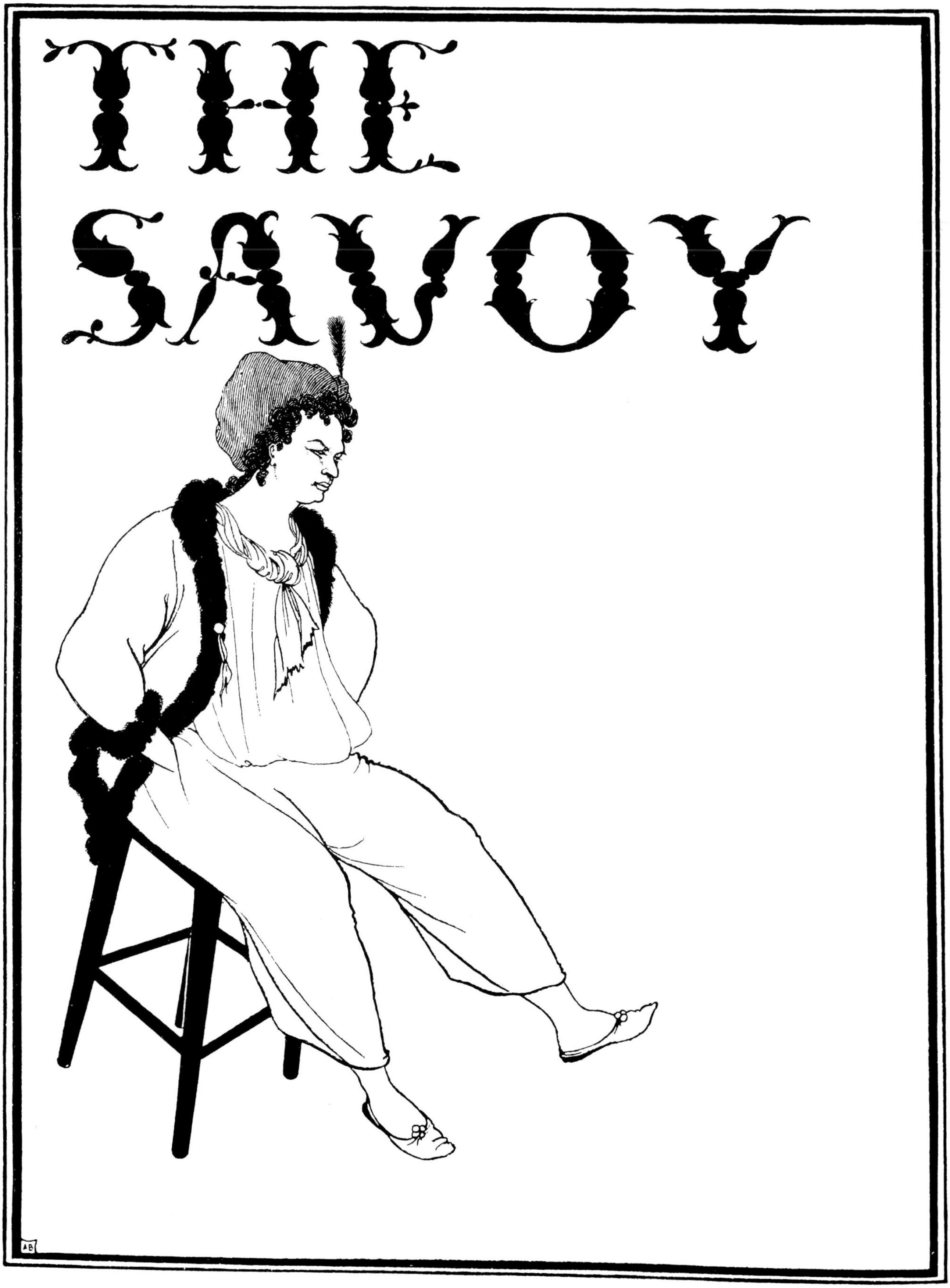
THE
SAVOY
AB

97. A Répétition of Tristan und Isolde. From The Savoy No. 8. 1896. A drawing of subtle values. In the last issue of The Savoy the artist issued twelve new drawings.

98. Don Juan, Sganarelle and the Beggar. From The Savoy No. 8. 1896.
The drawing was probably intended to illustrate a book to be published by
Smithers.

99. Mrs. Pinchwife. From The Savoy No. 8. 1896. Probably intended for an edition of Wycherley's Country Wife.

MRS PINCHWIFE

100. The Comedy of the Rhinegold. From The Savoy No. 8. 1896. A beautiful frontispiece, never completed, to an edition of Wagner's Opera. The three Rhine maidens are a complete contrast to the female types he drew for The Yellow Book.

THE
COMEDY
OF
THE
RHINEGOLD

101. Flosshilde.   From The Savoy No. 8.   1896.
Another drawing for his proposed illustrated edition of
Das Rheingold. It has been used as a bookplate.

102. Alberich. From The Savoy No. 8. 1896. Another drawing for Das Rheingold. It has the charm of a Japanese netsuke and reminds one of an earlier drawing The Glutton in Hell.

ALBERICH

103. Felix Mendelssohn Bartholdy.   From The Savoy No. 8. 1896.
One of a series of proposed caricatures of musicians.

104. Count Valmont. From The Savoy No. 8. 1896. Proposed titlepage to Les Liaisons Dangereuses.

LES
LIAISONS DANGEREUSES.

BY
CHODERLOS
DE LACLOS

AB

110. Cover design for Dowson's Verses. 1896. Smithers.
A simple but perfect cover design.

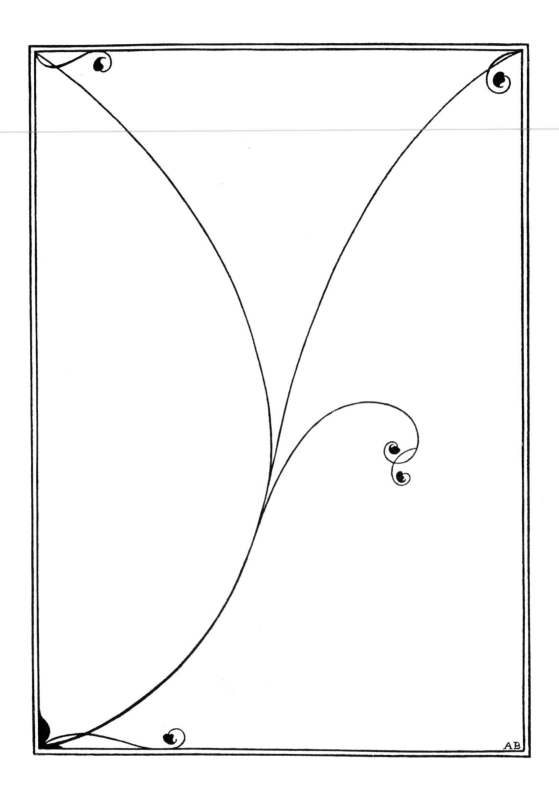

III. Frontispiece to The Pierrot of the Minute. 1897. Smithers. A lovely drawing with something of the quality of the Rape of the Lock series. It is surprising to learn it was made with little enthusiasm for Dowson's play.

112. Headpiece to The Pierrot of the Minute. 1897.
Smithers. Dowson's play was the last book for which he
made a complete series of illustrations before he died.

113. Cul-de-lampe to The Pierrot of the Minute. 1897. Smithers. A charming tailpiece to Ernest Dowson's Eighteenth Century fantasy.

114. Cover Design to The Pierrot of the Minute. 1897. Smithers. One of the most beautiful of his many brilliant cover designs. The upward swing of the figure has an almost Eastern rhythm, noticeable in many of his drawings.

THE
PIERROT
OF
THE
MINVTE.

115. Cover Design for A Book of Fifty Drawings. 1897. Smithers. This was the first collection of his drawings, followed, after his death, by A Second Book of Fifty Drawings.

A BOOK OF FIFTY DRAWINGS

BY

AVBREY BEARDSLEY

AVBREY
BEARDSLEY

LONDON
LEONARD SMITHERS
ROYAL ARCADE. W
1897.

116. Aubrey Beardsley's Book-Plate. 1897. Not used by the artist, but adapted by Mr H. A. Pollitt.

117. Ali Baba. Cover Design for a proposed edition of The Forty Thieves. 1897.
One of his most splendid covers, sparkling with colour.

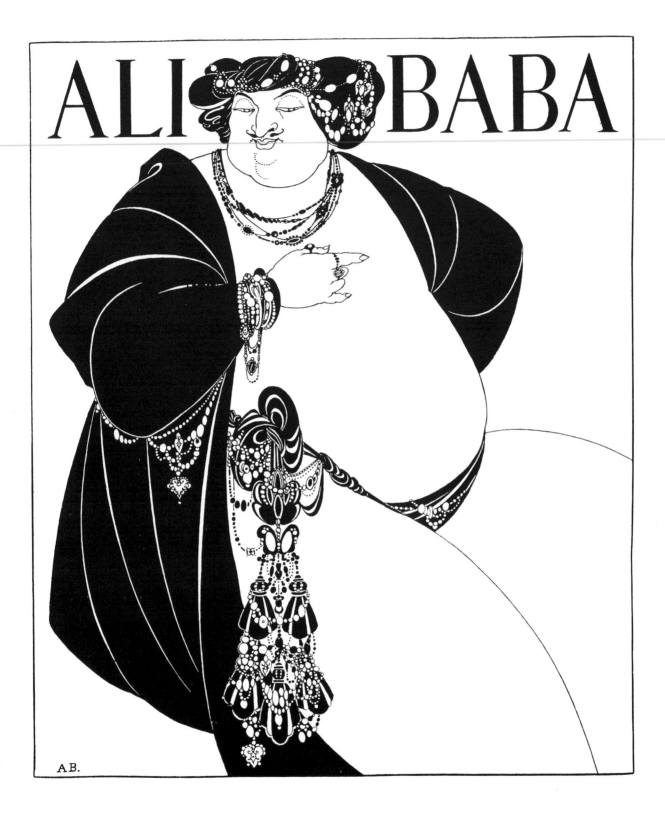

118. Ali Baba in the Wood. 1897. For a proposed edition of The Forty Thieves.

119. Atalanta II. 1897. A similar subject to the drawing intended for Vol. V of The Yellow Book, but not so used.

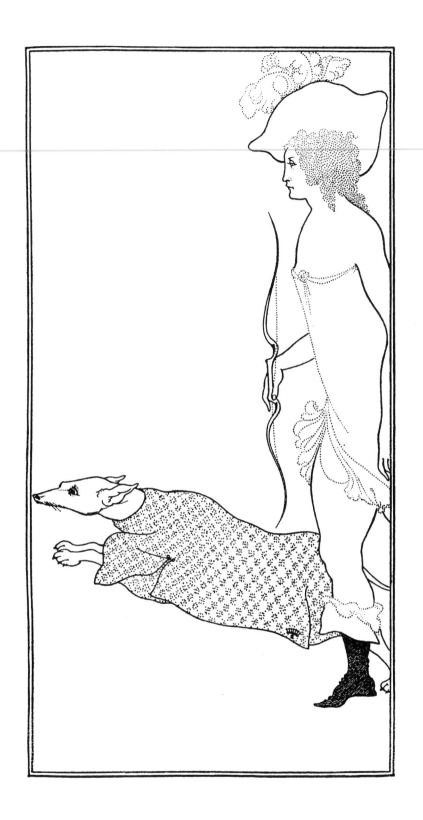

120. Messalina returning from the Bath. 1897. Probably intended as an illustration to the VI Satire of Juvenal. He made another drawing of the same subject with two figures.

MESSALINA.

121. Book-Plate of Olive Custance (Lady Alfred Douglas). 1897.

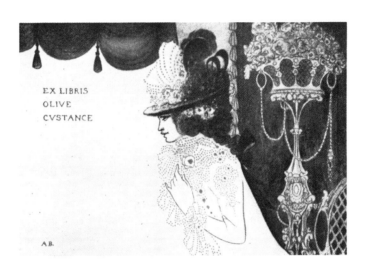

122. Mademoiselle de Maupin. 1897. For an intended edition of the book by Théophile Gautier, but published in a portfolio after the death of the artist.

123. D'Albert. 1897. For Mademoiselle de Maupin.
Executed in pen and wash.

124. D'Albert in Search of his Ideals. 1897. For Mademoiselle de Maupin. An example of his many delightful costume designs.

125. The Lady with the Rose. 1897. Included in the Mademoiselle de Maupin Portfolio but possibly not intended as an illustration.

126. Cover Design to The Houses of Sin. By Vincent O'Sullivan. 1897. Smithers. Printed on vellum in gold.

127. Arbuscula. 1897. An illustration to A History of Dancing by Gaston Vuillier. 1898. Heinemann.

128. Cover Design to Volpone by Ben Jonson. 1898. Smithers. The artist's last and in some ways best cover design. Although dated Paris 1898, it was finished in December 1897, at Mentone.

130. Initial Letter S (Vulture) to Volpone. 1898. Smithers. This and the following four initials are the artist's last work. They are executed in pencil and pen and are all he lived to finish out of twenty-four contemplated drawings.

134. Initial Letter V (Elephant) to Volpone. 1898.

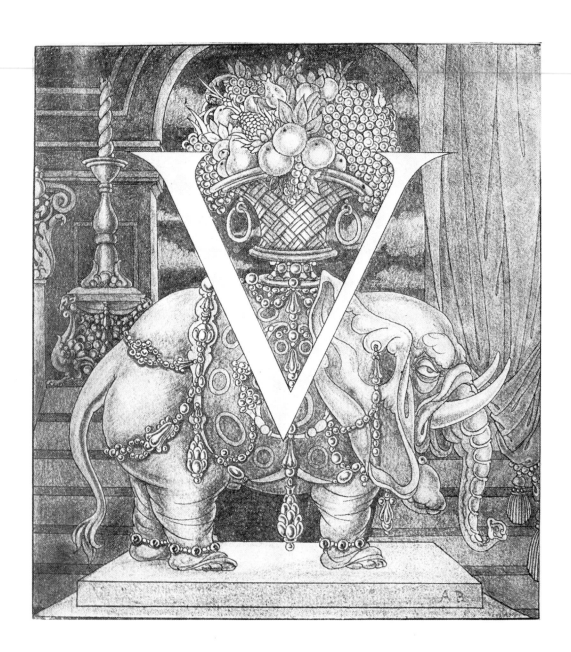

Acknowledgements

The Editor and Publishers acknowledge the courtesy of the following private collectors and public institutions who have kindly permitted reproductions to be made from the original drawings in their possession: The Fogg Museum of Art, Harvard University, for Maîtresse d'Orchestre (Salome, on Settle), The Stomach Dance, The Dancer's Reward, John and Salome, The Woman in the Moon, The Peacock Skirt, The Eyes of Herod, Tailpiece from Salome, The Mysterious Rose Garden, L'Education Sentimentale, Earl Lavender, A Chopin Nocturne, Frontispiece and Title Page for Venus and Tannhauser, Isolde, The New Star, Title Page to Savoy No. 1, Cover Design for Savoy No. 1, Felix Mendelssohn Bartholdy, Mademoiselle de Maupin, D'Albert in Search of his Ideals, and five Initials for Volpone; Mr. Scofield Thayer for Café Noir, The Baron's Prayer, Contents Page of Savoy No. 1, Savoy Prospectus Design, The Fruit Bearers, Alberich, Don Juan, Sganarelle and the Beggar, Cover Design for Savoy No. 8, Aubrey Beardsley's Book-Plate, Ali Baba in the Wood, The Lady with the Rose and Volpone Cover Design; The Boston Museum of Fine Arts for The Cave of Spleen; Mr. T. Tyler Sweeny, Jun. for Enter Herodias; The British Museum for The Toilet of Salome; The Victoria and Albert Museum for The Wagnerites and The Mirror of Love; Mr. Morton H. Sands for Chopin Ballade III, The Fourth Tableau of Das Rheingold and a Répétition of Tristan und Isolde; Mr. Martin Dent for The Return of Tannhauser to the Venusberg; Mrs. Hippisley Cox for Design for the Princes Ladies' Golf Club Card; The Brighton Art Gallery for Design for Yellow Book Vol. V.

The Publishers also wish to acknowledge with gratitude the kindness of Messrs. J. M. Dent & Sons, Ltd. in lending certain photographs and blocks.

Index